100
Fat-free Recipes

Elizabeth Jyothi Mathew
*Culinary expert and a regular cookery columnist
and contributor to magazines*

Published by:

F-2/16, Ansari road, Daryaganj, New Delhi-110002
☏ 23240026, 23240027 • *Fax:* 011-23240028
Email: info@vspublishers.com • *Website:* www.vspublishers.com

Branch : Hyderabad
5-1-707/1, Brij Bhawan (Beside Central Bank of India Lane)
Bank Street, Koti Hyderabad - 500 095
☏ 040-24737290
E-mail: vspublishershyd@gmail.com

Distributors :

▶ **Pustak Mahal®**, Delhi
J-3/16, Daryaganj, New Delhi-110002
☏ 23276539, 23272783, 23272784 • *Fax:* 011-23260518
E-mail: sales@pustakmahal.com • *Website:* www.pustakmahal.com
Bengaluru: ☏ 080-22234025 • *Telefax:* 080-22240209
Patna: ☏ 0612-3294193 • *Telefax:* 0612-2302719

▶ **PM Publications**
- 10-B, Netaji Subhash Marg, Daryaganj, New Delhi-110002
  ☏ 23268292, 23268293, 23279900 • *Fax:* 011-23280567
  E-mail: pmpublications@gmail.com
- 6686, Khari Baoli, Delhi-110006
  ☏ 23944314, 23911979

▶ **Unicorn Books**
Mumbai :
23-25, Zaoba Wadi (Opp. VIP Showroom), Thakurdwar, Mumbai-400002
☏ 022-22010941 • *Telefax:* 022-22053387

© **Copyright:**
ISBN 978-93-813842-8-2
Edition : 2011

The Copyright of this book, as well as all matter contained herein (including illustrations) rests with the Publishers. No person shall copy the name of the book, its title design, matter and illustrations in any form and in any language, totally or partially or in any distorted form. Anybody doing so shall face legal action and will be responsible for damages.

Printed at : Param Offsetters, Okhla, New Delhi

*Dedicated to my Lord and Saviour
Jesus Christ, without whom my life
would have had no meaning*

Acknowledgements

First and foremost my deepest gratitude to Jesus Christ without whom nothing would have been possible.

Thanks to God's blessings in my life, my husband, Dr Mathew Abraham, and our children Satshya, Prethyash and Sneha for encouraging me and giving me the motivation to experiment with new dishes.

Thanks to my parents, Mrs and Dr John Jacob and Mrs and Dr Kurien Abraham, for being the best parents in the world.

Thanks to Mrs and Mr Jacob Cheriyan (Australia), Mrs and Dr Kurien P Abraham, Mrs and Mr John Thomas, Mrs and Dr Tony George (USA) for their love and support.

Thanks to all my family members and friends, in India and in Singapore. May God bless you all!

—Elizabeth Jyothi Mathew

This is my commandment, that you love one another as I have loved you.

—John 15:12

Preface

In this fast-moving day and age, it has become a necessity to be as healthy as possible. One of the ways to maintain a healthy lifestyle is by cooking food that is nutritious as well as low in calories. It does not mean that watching one's diet means good food has to be sacrificed. This is the aim of every cook who wants to maintain a figure as well as eat exotic food with lesser calories.

The book has been written with the aim that the reader will embark on a journey of experimenting with the different recipes and incorporate them into a lifestyle that is healthy. These are all calorie-counted recipes to help you maintain a diet that includes all types of food. It is my hope and endeavour that you have fun trying out these recipes, which will allow you to embark on a journey of a lifetime. Remember – you are very special because God created you. He loves you, so keep smiling!

All suggestions and comments are welcome on my e-mail address: *ktm_matjothi@sancharnet.in*.

God bless!

—**Elizabeth Jyothi Mathew**

Contents

Vegetable Dishes 11
Cucumber Potato Salad 11
Yoghurt Dressing 12
Easy Mixed Salad 13
Breakfast Beans 14
Mushroom Pate 15
Carrot and Orange Soup 16
Red Cabbage Stir-fry 17
Garden Vegetable Dip 18
Grilled Peppers 19
Lemon Broccoli 20
Orange and Mushroom Salad 21
French Dressing 22
Quick and Easy Macaroni Salad 23
Ratatouille 24
Tropical Bean Sprout Coleslaw 25
Easy Vegetable Bake 26
Cottage Cheese, Fruit and Sprout Salad 27
Quick and Easy Stir-fry 28
Sunshine Dip 29
Healthy Tomato Salad 30
Novelty Mushrooms 31
German Potato Salad 32
Garlic Mashed Potatoes 33

Mexican Beans and Rice	34
Macaroni, Corn and Tomato Salad	35
Potato and Cucumber Salad	36
Quick Thousand Island Dressing	37
Rice Salad with Baby Vegetables	38
Rice Combination Salad	39
Hash Brown Casserole	40
Glazed Carrots	41
Baked Spicy Fries	42
Oriental Mushroom and Paneer Delight	43
Mediterranean Eggplant Casserole	45
Broccoli and Cheese Casserole	47
Spicy Salsa	48
Garlic Green Beans	49
Potato Delight	50
Layered Salad	51
Warm Potato Salad	52
Party Stuffed Mushrooms	53
Cool Cucumber Salad	54
Low-fat Ranch Dressing with Herbs	55
Eggplant with Roasted Peanuts	56
Baked Corn on the Cob	58
Potatoes Lyonnaise	59
Tomato and Onion Grill	60
Cucumber and Celery Filling	61
Stuffed Mushrooms	62
Yummy Stuffed Potatoes	63
Potato Cheese Hash	64
Brazilian Salad	65
Mushroom and Cheese Salad	66

Simple Potato Salad 67
Simple Relish 68
Easy Mint Chutney 69

Meat and Poultry Dishes 70
Cheese Chicken Drumsticks 70
Simple Bread Pizza 71
Sunset Stir-fry 72
Honey Mustard Chicken 73
Chicken Drumsticks 74
Roast Lemon Chicken 75
Chicken, Mushroom and Pineapple Salad 76
Chicken Kebabs 77
Barbecued Chicken 78
Honey Chicken 79
Chicken Soufflé 80
Orange Glazed Chicken Tenders 81
Lamb Meatballs 82
Caribbean Chicken 83

Seafood Dishes..84
Salmon Mousse 84
Simple Salmon 85
Tuna Pate 86
Honey Sardines 87
Surprise Fish Parcels 88
Baked Whole Fish with Vegetable Stuffing 89
Fish Turbans 91
Fish Bean Steak 92
Asian Stir-fry 93
Oriental Fish 94
Mustard Tuna 95

Barbecued Fish with
Mushroom Stuffing 96
Delicious Tuna Filling 97
Special Stuffed Tomatoes 98
Chilled Prawns 99
Peppered Fish Kebabs 100
Grape and Prawn Fresh Salad 101
Greek Fish Starter 102
Barbecued Fish 103

Desserts 104
Nutty Peaches 104
Apple Delight with Custard Sauce 105
Luscious Strawberry Whip 107
Baked Pineapple 108
Dreamy Tropical Pineapple and Lychee 109
Easy Spice Biscuits 110
Banana Muffins 111
Low-calorie Banana Delight 112
Watermelon Surprise 113
Light Crème Brulee 114
Banana Raisin Muffins 115
Pineapple Upside-down Cake 116

Vegetable Dishes

Cucumber Potato Salad

(Serves 4 persons)

Easy to make, easy to serve and easy on the tummy!

Ingredients
- 2 cucumbers
- ½ kg potatoes, washed
- 1 cup yoghurt
- Mint leaves

Method

Cook the potatoes in salted water and peel after cooling. Cut into slices. Peel cucumber and cut into slices. In a salad bowl, put one layer of potatoes and one layer of cucumber and sprinkle yoghurt dressing on it. Continue layering and sprinkle the mint leaves. Leave for at least half an hour and serve.

117 calories per serving

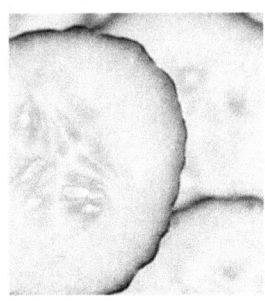

Yoghurt Dressing

(Serves 4 persons)

Want a dressing that's simple yet delicious? Try this and add spunk to your dish.

Ingredients
- ½ litre yoghurt
- 2 tsp olive oil
- Juice of 1 lemon
- Salt and pepper to taste

Method
Mix all the ingredients in a blender. Taste and season.

1 tbsp = 34 calories

Easy Mixed Salad

(Serves 4 persons)

Watch your calorie intake with this good mix of vegetables and healthy dressing.

Ingredients
- 1 lettuce, washed and chopped roughly
- ½ kg carrot, peeled and grated
- ½ kg cucumber, sliced
- 2 apples, peeled and cut into thin strips
-   kg red cabbage, chopped finely
- 1 cup yoghurt dressing

Method
Mix all the ingredients for the salad together. Add the yoghurt dressing and toss well. Put into a salad bowl and sprinkle with chopped mint leaves.

51 calories per serving

Breakfast Beans

(Serves 4 persons)

Start your day with this healthy breakfast and feel great!

Ingredients
- 1 tsp oil
- 2 onions, chopped
- 6 medium tomatoes, chopped
- 2 tsp coriander leaves, chopped
- 1½ cup kidney beans
- Salt and pepper to taste

Method

Heat the oil in a non-stick frying pan. Add onions and fry till soft and golden. Add the tomatoes and cook, stirring occasionally until mixture is reduced to a smooth puree. Add the coriander leaves and simmer for about 15 minutes. Remove from heat and serve hot or cold with fresh bread or toast. Garnish with extra coriander leaves.

130 calories per serving

Mushroom Pate

(Serves 4 persons)

This is good as a snack or even as a main meal.

Ingredients
- 2 onions, finely chopped
- 500 gm mushroom, finely sliced
- 1 tbsp oil
- 1 tbsp coriander leaves
- 3 tsp coriander powder
- Chilli sauce, if needed
- Salt and pepper to taste

Method
Heat oil in frying pan and sauté onions and mushrooms, stirring for 20 minutes. Mix coriander powder with coriander leaves and wheat germ and add to the mushroom mixture. Add few drops of chilli sauce and bake in oiled terrine for about one hour at 200 C. Serve with dry biscuits or toast.

350 calories per recipe

Carrot and Orange Soup

(Serves 6 persons)

Try this soup with a difference!

Ingredients
- 2 tsp oil
- 400 gm carrots, chopped
- 1 large onion, chopped
- Juice of 2 oranges
- 1 tsp grated orange rind
- 1 litre chicken stock
- 1 crushed clove garlic
- Freshly ground pepper
- 6 tbsp non-fat yoghurt
- 6 thin slices of orange and mint to garnish

Method
Heat oil; then add carrots and onions. Cook gently for 10 minutes and add juice, rind, stock, garlic and pepper. Simmer for about 15 minutes until carrots are tender. Blend in a mixer. Serve hot or chilled with a spoonful of yoghurt. Garnish with thin slice of orange and mint.

55 calories per serving

Red Cabbage Stir-fry

(Serves 4 persons)

Make this dish close to serving time.

Ingredients

- 300 gm broccoli
- 1 tbsp oil
- 1 medium green pepper, chopped
- 2 green shallots, chopped
- 150 gm mushrooms, sliced
- ½ kg red cabbage, finely shredded
- ⅓ cup roasted, salted cashew-nuts
- 1 tbsp light soya sauce
- 2 tsp corn flour, mixed with 2 tsp water
- 2 cups bean sprouts

Method

Cut broccoli into flowerets. Heat oil in a large frying pan. Add broccoli, pepper, shallots, garlic and mushrooms. Stir-fry over high heat for about 2 to 3 minutes. Add cabbage and nuts and stir-fry for a further minute. Stir in the soya sauce and corn flour mixture. Stir-fry over heat till sauce boils. Quickly stir in the bean sprouts and serve.

196 calories per serving

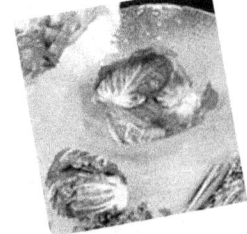

Garden Vegetable Dip

(Serves 4 persons)

This dip is good with biscuits and toast.

Ingredients
- 16 oz low-fat cottage cheese (paneer)
- cup broccoli, chopped
- cup carrot, finely chopped
- 2 tbsp green onion, chopped
- 1 tbsp coriander leaves, chopped
- 2 tbsp parsley, chopped
- 2 tsp mayonnaise

Method
Blend cottage cheese in blender or food processor till pureed. Then spoon into another bowl and stir in remaining ingredients. Mix well and refrigerate for several hours till chilled. This is a good dip to serve with vegetables, crackers or toast. The filling can also be used for sandwiches.

20 calories per serving

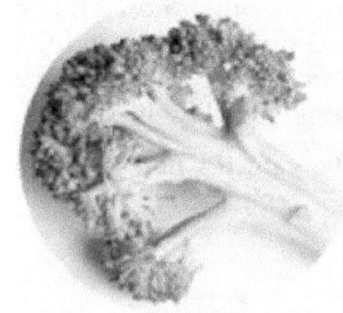

Grilled Peppers

(Serves 2 persons)

This is very easy to make as a delicious side dish.

Ingredients

- 2 large red peppers
- 2 green peppers (capsicum)
- 1 medium onion, finely chopped
- 6 tbsp French dressing (*recipe given below*)

Method

Cut each pepper into half vertically. Grill until the skins begin to blacken. Remove from grill and peel off skins. Slice into quarters and remove all seeds and pith. Next, mix peppers with onion and place in a small dish. Pour French dressing over warm peppers and marinate for another 30 minutes. Serve with meat chops or sausages.

237 calories

French dressing:

Mix together 2 tbsp vinegar, 6 tbsp olive oil, single crushed garlic clove, salt and pepper.

Lemon Broccoli

(Serves 4 persons)

Feeling hungry and worried about calories? Make this easy dish and feel great!

Ingredients

- 500 gm broccoli
- 1 tbsp lemon juice
- Freshly ground black pepper
- Salt to taste

Method

Wash broccoli and split into florets. Steam, boil or microwave broccoli in small quantity of water. When tender, drain and add lemon juice mixed with salt and pepper. Toss in pan gently and serve hot.

30 calories per serving

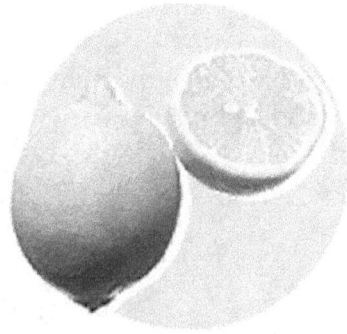

Orange and Mushroom Salad

(Serves 4 persons)

This is a light and refreshing salad that will increase your zest for the new day!

Ingredients

- 3 oranges, peeled and cut into segments
- 1½ cup sliced mushrooms
- ½ cucumber, seeds removed and coarsely grated
- 4 shallots, finely chopped
- 2 tbsp French dressing (*recipe given on next page*)

Method

Place all ingredients in a bowl and toss lightly. Chill and serve.

55 calories per serving

French Dressing

(Serves 4 persons)

Though made with the simplest of ingredients, this dressing really makes the salad worth serving.

Ingredients
- 1 tbsp oil
- 3 tbsp vinegar
- ½ tsp ground pepper
- ½ tsp mustard powder
- 1 clove garlic, crushed

Method
Place all ingredients in a screw-top jar and shake well. Larger quantities can be made and stored in refrigerator. Serve with salad.

180 calories

Quick and Easy Macaroni Salad

(Serves 4–6 persons)

This is really easy to make and will satisfy any hungry person!

Ingredients
- 2 cups cooked cold macaroni or any pasta
- 1 cup cooked mixed vegetables (carrots, beans etc)
- 1 cucumber, chopped
- cup toasted almonds
- 1 tsp chopped coriander leaves
- 200 gm non-fat yoghurt

Method
Mix all ingredients together and decorate with extra coriander leaves.

215 calories per serving

Alternatively 1 cup of cooked chicken or lean meat can be mixed with the pasta to make a light meal.

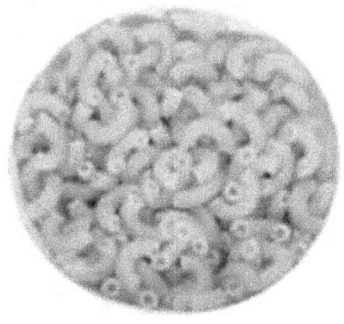

Ratatouille

(Serves 4 persons)

Talk about fat-free, healthy yet tasty. This dish certainly takes the honours!

Ingredients

- 1 capsicum
- 1 small eggplant
- 2 small cucumbers
- 1 large onion
- 1 large tomato, chopped
- Salt and pepper to taste
- 1 tsp oil

Method

Remove seeds and pith from capsicum and cut into rings. Wash eggplant and cucumber and cut into 1-cm slices. Heat heavy-base saucepan and add oil, garlic, onion and capsicum and cook gently for several minutes. Add eggplant, cucumber, tomato, oregano and cover. Simmer for about 10 minutes. Remove lid and continue cooking for another 5 to 10 minutes to reduce the liquid.

40 calories per serving

Tropical Bean Sprout Coleslaw

(Serves 4 persons)

This is a light and satisfying salad enjoyed by one and all!

Ingredients
- 5 oz bean sprouts
- 1 cup cabbage, sliced
- ½ cup seedless grapes cut in half
- ½ cup fresh pineapple

Dressing:
- ½ cup low-fat yoghurt
- 1 tsp mustard
-   cup mayonnaise
- Salt to taste

Method
Mix bean sprouts, cabbage, grapes and pineapple in a bowl. Lightly mix in the ingredients in the dressing and serve with salad greens.

102 calories per serving

Easy Vegetable Bake

(Serves 2 persons)

Made with the simplest of ingredients, this bake will definitely be an easy one to make.

Ingredients
- 1 cucumber, cut into pieces
- 2 tomatoes, sliced
- 1 tbsp coriander leaves
- 1 egg
- 2 tsp olive oil
- 2 oz low-fat cheese, grated
- Salt and pepper to taste

Method
Preheat oven. In ovenproof dish, mix all ingredients together except for the egg and cheese. Bake for about 20 minutes till cucumbers are golden brown. Push vegetables to the side of the dish to make a well in the centre. Carefully crack egg into the hole and sprinkle over cheese. Bake for a further 10 minutes or until the egg is cooked to your liking. Serve hot with salad.

225 calories per serving

Cottage Cheese, Fruit and Sprout Salad

(Serves 2 persons)

This is a dish that's light on the tummy.

Ingredients
- ½ cup low-fat cottage cheese (paneer)
- ½ cup sprouts
- 4 tbsp pineapple, chopped
- 4 tbsp mango, chopped
- 2 lettuce leaves

Method
Mix cottage cheese (paneer) and sprouts. Add pineapple and mango. Serve chilled on lettuce leaves.

78 calories

Quick and Easy Stir-fry

(Serves 4 persons)

It's better to eat this piping hot!

Ingredients
- 1 tbsp oil
- 1 tbsp garlic, chopped
- 1 onion, sliced thinly
- 1 stalk celery, sliced
- 1 cup mushroom, sliced
- 12 oz bean sprouts
- ½ tsp ginger, chopped
- 1 tsp oyster sauce
- 2 tsp light soya sauce

Method
Prepare and set aside all ingredients. In a large skillet or wok, heat oil. Add garlic, onion, celery and cook for a minute. Add mushroom and bean sprouts. Add sauces and stir-fry. Serve over hot rice.

157 calories

Sunshine Dip

(Serves 4 persons)

This dip is somewhat different because both Western and Indian ingredients are blended together.

Ingredients

- 1 small cauliflower, steamed till soft
- Juice of 1 lemon
- ½ tsp curry powder
- 1 pinch cardamom powder
- ⅓ cup mayonnaise
- 1 cup sprouts
- 2 carrots, grated
- 2 tomatoes, sliced

Method

Mash cauliflower and all ingredients listed till the mayonnaise. Mix well. Add the sprouts, carrots and tomatoes and serve with *chapattis*.

171 calories

Healthy Tomato Salad

(Serves 4 persons)

This looks very pretty when served in capsicum shells!

Ingredients
- 4 cups tomatoes, chopped
- 1 cup spring onions, chopped
- ½ tbsp olive oil
- ½ cup vinegar
- 1 cup coriander leaves
- 1 green pepper
- Salt and pepper to taste

Method
Mix tomatoes, spring onions and leaves. Whisk together olive oil, vinegar, salt and pepper. Pour over salad mixture and mix. Marinate for about half an hour. Cut green pepper into two vertically. Remove seeds and fill each half with salad mixture. Serve.

54 calories

Novelty Mushrooms

(Serves 4 persons)

Try this novelty combination of bacon and mushrooms. The two go together like Jack and Jill!

Ingredients

- 3 cups mushrooms
- 1 cup bacon, chopped
- 20 gm butter
- 3 eggs
- 2 tbsp skimmed milk
- Coriander leaves to decorate

Method

Preheat oven. Dry-fry bacon in non-stick pan till crisp. Brush mushrooms with little bacon fat and bake in oven for about 5 to 10 minutes. Meanwhile, heat butter in saucepan. Beat eggs and milk together and pour into saucepan. Make light and fluffy scrambled eggs. Drain any extra liquid from the pan. Stir in the cooked bacon. Arrange in a plate and place oven-baked mushrooms on top. Sprinkle some coriander leaves and serve.

178 calories

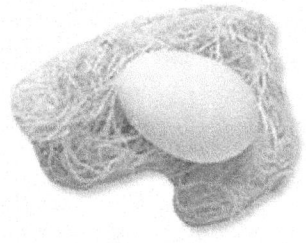

German Potato Salad

(Serves 4 persons)

Bacon and potatoes are a good combination and worth the effort!

Ingredients

- kg potatoes, boiled till just tender
- 2 slices bacon, chopped
- 1 tbsp flour
- 1 tsp sugar
- cup vinegar
- ⅓ cup hot water
- ⅓ cup spring onions, chopped
- Salt and pepper to taste

Method

Cook bacon in non-stick pan till crispy. Add flour and stir for a minute. Combine sugar, hot water and vinegar and add to bacon mixture. Cook stirring constantly until sauce thickens. Drain potatoes, cool, peel and slice. Add to sauce along with onion, salt and pepper. Serve warm or chilled.

157 calories

Garlic Mashed Potatoes

(Serves 4 persons)

If you feel like trying something somewhat on the heavier side, try this.

Ingredients

- 3 large potatoes
- 2 cups skim milk
- 3 cloves garlic, smashed
- 1 tsp white pepper
- Salt to taste

Method

Cover and cook potatoes in a small amount of boiling water until tender. Remove from heat. Drain and cover. Meanwhile, in a small saucepan over low heat, cook garlic in milk for about 20 minutes until garlic is soft. Add garlic-milk mixture and pepper to potatoes. Mash with potato masher till smooth. Serve with meat roast and baked vegetables.

141 calories

Mexican Beans and Rice

(Serves 4–6 persons)

Here is some Mexican stuff for a change...

Ingredients
- 1 cup long-grain rice, cooked
- 1 tsp olive oil
- 1 cup onion, chopped
- 1 cup celery, sliced
- 1 clove garlic, minced
- 15 oz red beans, cooked
- 8 oz tomato sauce
- ½ cup water
- 2 tsp chilli powder
- ½ tsp chilli flakes
- 1 tsp pepper

Method
Cook the rice in a pan, heat oil and add onions. Stir and add celery and garlic. Cook and stir until crisp and tender. Add beans, tomato sauce, water, chilli powder, chilli flakes and pepper. Heat thoroughly, stirring occasionally. Serve over hot rice.

206 calories

Macaroni, Corn and Tomato Salad

(Serves 4–6 persons)

This can be prepared four hours before and stored in the refrigerator.

Ingredients
- cup uncooked macaroni
- 4 medium tomatoes cut into thin wedges
- 5 green onions, thinly sliced
- 1 cup halved cucumber, thinly sliced
- 1 cup corn kernels
- 1 cup coriander leaves, chopped
- ⅓ cup plain, non-fat yoghurt
- 3 tbsp low-fat mayonnaise
- 2 tbsp fresh lemon juice
- 2 garlic cloves, chopped

Method
Cook macaroni in boiling water till tender. Drain and rinse under cold water, then place macaroni in large bowl. Add tomato, green onions, cucumber and corn. Combine the leaves, yoghurt, mayonnaise, lemon juice and garlic in a bowl. Mix well. Next, mix this with the macaroni mixture and toss well. Add salt and pepper to taste.

189 calories

Potato and Cucumber Salad

(Serves 4 persons)

Garnish salad with lot of coriander and mint leaves.

Ingredients
- kg potatoes
- ½ cup plain non-fat yoghurt
- 1 tbsp fresh coriander leaves
- ½ tsp ground coriander seeds
- 1 tbsp fresh lemon juice
- 1 large cucumber, seeded and cut into half-inch cubes

Method
Peel potatoes and cut into half-inch cubes. Cook potatoes until tender in large saucepan of boiling salted water for about 5 minutes. Drain potatoes and rinse under cold water in colander. Drain potatoes well. Stir together yoghurt, dill, coriander and lemon juice in a small bowl. Combine with potatoes, cucumber and season well with salt and pepper. Toss to coat.

121 calories

Quick Thousand Island Dressing

(Serves 4 persons)

This is good to make and store in the refrigerator for those last-minute guests!

Ingredients

- ⅓ cup low-fat mayonnaise
- 2 tbsp ketchup
- 2 tbsp lemon juice
- 2 tbsp minced red or green pepper
- 1 tbsp onion, minced
- 1 tbsp coriander leaves, minced
- 1 tbsp sweet pickle relish
- Salt and pepper to taste
- cup water

Method

Blend all ingredients and salt to taste in a blender or food processor until smooth, adding up to 2 tbsp additional water, if needed, to a thin dressing of desired consistency. Covered and chilled, dressing keeps for one week. Serve with sliced tomatoes, crisp lettuce or seafood salad. This makes about one cup.

1 tbsp = 12 calories (approx.)

Rice Salad with Baby Vegetables

(Serves 4–6 persons)

Baby ingredients for tiny kids!

Ingredients

- 4 oz baby carrots (about 16), trimmed, halved lengthwise
- 8 oz baby cucumber, ends trimmed, halved
- cup long-grain white rice
- ½ cup plain low-fat yoghurt
- 3 tbsp chopped fresh coriander leaves
- 1½ tbsp rice vinegar
- 1 tsp olive oil
- Fresh mint leaves (optional)

Method

Blanch carrots in large pot of boiling salted water for one minute. Combine zucchini with carrots and cook for one minute. Transfer vegetables to colander using a slotted spoon. Rinse vegetables with cold water; drain well. Add rice to same pot of boiling water. Cook for 15 minutes or until tender. Drain. Rinse under cold water; drain well. Cool to room temperature. Combine rice, carrots and zucchini in large bowl. Toss in yoghurt, chopped dill, vinegar and oil. Add salt and pepper to taste. Garnish with mint leaves.

173 calories

Rice Combination Salad

(Serves 4 persons)

Feel like splurging with rice served in a different way? Try this. It is fruity and light – a delight for all!

Ingredients

- 225 gm Biryani rice
- 12 whole cardamom pods
- 1 cup pineapple pieces, chopped
- ½ cucumber, peeled and diced
- 50 gm nuts, roasted
- Salt and pepper to taste

Dressing:

- Juice of 1 orange
- 6 tbsp vegetable oil
- 1 tsp coriander powder
- 1 tsp chilli powder

Method

Cook rice with cardamom pods in a pan of boiling salted water. Drain rice and rinse with iced water. Add pineapple, cucumber and nuts and mix well. Mix all dressing ingredients well and pour over the rice and toss gently so that all ingredients are well coated. Serve sprinkled with coriander leaves.

500 calories

Hash Brown Casserole

(Serves 4–6 persons)

Honey, cornflakes and potato make this a special dish!

Ingredients

- 4 cups potatoes, grated
- ½ cup onions, chopped
- 5 oz cream of mushroom soup
- ⅓ cup honey
- Salt and pepper to taste
- 1 pint fat-free sour cream
- 1 cup fat-free cheese, shredded
- cup reduced fat margarine, melted
- 1 cup cornflakes

Method

Preheat oven. Grease a baking dish and set aside. In non-stick pan, cook potato with some margarine. Combine potato, onions, soup, honey, salt, black pepper, sour cream and cheese in a large mixing bowl. Mix well. Spoon mixture into prepared pan.

Combine melted margarine and cornflakes in a small bowl. Stir together. Top evenly over casserole. Bake for 45 minutes.

182 calories

Glazed Carrots

(Serves 4 persons)

This dish has a sweet taste.

Ingredients
- ½ kg baby carrots
- 1 tbsp butter
- 2 tbsp brown sugar
- ½ cup apple juice
- 2 tbsp fresh ginger
- tsp cumin, toasted in hot oven
- 1 tsp white pepper
- Pinch of salt

Method
In boiling water, cook carrots for about 10 minutes or until tender. Let carrots cool. Melt butter and sugar in a pot. Stir frequently. Reduce heat and cook for 5 minutes to caramelise and then remove from heat. Add juice, bring to boil and reduce heat. Liquid will be light syrup. Add carrots, ginger and cumin to the liquid. Stir. Cook mixture on medium heat until glazed. Add salt and pepper.

110 calories per serving

Baked Spicy Fries

(Serves 4 persons)

Do you have a craving for French fries but don't want all that oil? Try this out and skip the oil.

Ingredients
- 6 medium baking potatoes
- 1 tbsp olive oil
- ½ tbsp chilli powder
- 3 tsp pepper

Method
Cut potatoes into wedges or slices and lightly grease a baking sheet with oil. Place potato wedges or slices in a plastic bag with spices and half of the oil, then toss to cover all. Bake at 350 F for about 45 minutes turning and brushing often with the remaining oil. Broil for about 5 minutes, turning after 3 minutes.

185 calories

Oriental Mushroom and Paneer Delight

(Serves 4 persons)

Make this when you have time to spare.

Ingredients

- 2 cups mushrooms
- 1 onion, sliced in rings
- 2 cloves garlic
- 2 tbsp olive oil
- 1 tbsp coriander leaves
- Salt and pepper to taste
- 1 cup paneer, drained
- 1 cup low-fat sour cream
- 2 tbsp flour
- 1 tbsp grated orange peel
- 6 cups noodles, cooked and drained
- cup skim milk
- ½ green pepper, sliced

Method

Heat oil in a wok or large sauté pan over medium-high heat. Cook onion, garlic and mushrooms (reserving a few mushroom slices) in oil for 10 minutes, stirring often, until tender. Stir in coriander leaves, salt and pepper. As the mushrooms are cooking, place paneer, sour cream, milk and flour in blender. Cover and blend on medium until smooth. Stir this mixture over mushroom mixture and cook over medium heat, stirring constantly until the mixture is thickened. Place this entire mixture over hot cooked noodles and sprinkle orange peel. Sauté yellow pepper and reserved mushroom slices in a little oil until tender. Dot the top of the dish with these slices. For added colour place a few orange slices on platter just before serving.

385 calories

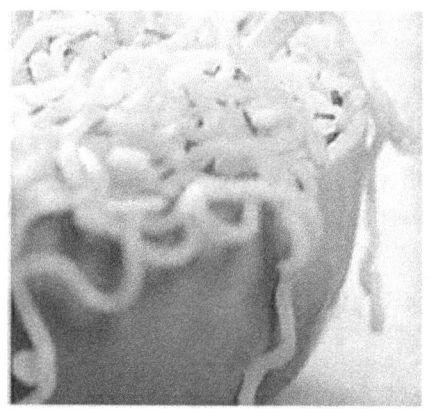

Mediterranean Eggplant Casserole

(Serves 4–6 persons)

Try this for a change and feel like you have travelled to the Mediterranean and back!

Ingredients

- 2 tsp olive oil
- 1 onion, halved and sliced
- 3 cloves garlic, minced
- 1 tsp coriander leaves
- Salt and pepper to taste
- 5 tomatoes, chopped
- 1 cup dry bread crumbs, seasoned
- cup grated Parmesan cheese, divided
- 3 egg whites, lightly beaten
- 1 cup mozzarella cheese, shredded
- 750 gm eggplant, peeled and cut crosswise into ⅜ inch thick slices

Method

Prepare a greased cookie sheet and set aside. Mix breadcrumbs with 2 tbsp of Parmesan cheese. Beat egg whites with ½ tsp salt. Dip eggplant slices in egg whites, coat with seasoned breadcrumbs. Place eggplant slices on prepared cookie sheet. You will have two different batches. Set aside. In non-stick skillet heat oil over medium heat, add onion and garlic. Cook until softened. Add coriander leaves, salt and pepper. Cook for one minute. Add tomatoes, increase heat to high and cook until thickened for about 10 to 12 minutes. Remove from heat.

Broil eggplant slices, one batch at a time for 3 to 5 minutes per side, until brown. Preheat oven to 425 F. Layer eggplant slices in a baking dish. Top with tomato mixture and sprinkle with mozzarella cheese and the remaining Parmesan cheese. Bake uncovered for 10 to 15 minutes until cheese is bubbly.

249 calories

Broccoli and Cheese Casserole

(Serves 4–6 persons)

Try this with bread – it's simply yummy!

Ingredients
- 30 oz broccoli, chopped
- 1 egg
- 1 packet mushroom soup, made into soup
- 1 cup fat-free mayonnaise
- ½ cup low-fat cheese, shredded
- 2 tbsp onions, minced
- Dash of black pepper
- 6 crackers, crushed

Method
Preheat oven to 350 F. Grease casserole dish. Set aside. Cook broccoli. Combine broccoli, egg, soup and mayonnaise in a large bowl. Stir. Add cheese, onions and pepper to broccoli mixture. Stir. Pour broccoli-cheese mixture into prepared casserole dish. Crush and sprinkle crackers over top of mixture. Bake at 350 F for about 30 minutes or until sauce is hot and bubbly.

153 calories

Spicy Salsa

(Serves 4–6 persons)

Make this a few hours before you serve and let the flavours seep in.

Ingredients
- cup chopped onion
- 8 tomatoes, chopped
- ½ red onion, diced
- 2 green peppers, diced pulp and seeds removed
- 2 cloves garlic, chopped
- cup fresh coriander leaves
- ½ tsp cumin
- cup lime juice
- Salt and fresh ground pepper to taste

Method
Combine all ingredients in a large plastic or glass bowl (not aluminium). Cover and let stand overnight in refrigerator.

25 calories

Garlic Green Beans

(Serves 4 persons)

Try this and fill your tummy. The best thing is you will not feel any guilt!

Ingredients

- ½ kg green beans, cleaned, with ends removed
- 1 tbsp salt
- 1 tbsp olive oil
- 2 to 3 tsp garlic, minced
- cup coriander leaves, chopped
- Salt and pepper to taste

Method

Bring a large pot of water to boil. Add one tablespoon of salt. Pour cleaned beans into pot. Cook green beans until tender, yet firm. Remove from pot and pour cold water over beans until they are cool.

Heat large sauté pan, then add oil and beans. Cook for 3 to 4 minutes. Add garlic and leaves and continue to cook until beans are hot. Season with salt and pepper.

60 calories

Potato Delight

(Serves 4–6 persons)

This is a definite delight!

Ingredients
- 6 medium potatoes
- 3 stalks broccoli
- cup skim milk
- 1 cup shredded Cheddar cheese
- 1/8 tsp pepper

Method
Scrub potatoes. Make shallow slits around the middle as if you were cutting the potatoes in half lengthwise. Bake 30 to 60 minutes until done, depending on size. Peel broccoli stems. Steam whole stalks just until tender and chop finely.

Carefully slice potatoes in half and scoop the insides into a bowl with the broccoli. Add milk, cup cheese and pepper. Mash together until the mixture is pale green with dark green flecks. Heap this into potato jackets and sprinkle with remaining cheese. Return to 350 F oven to heat for about 15 minutes.

315 calories

Layered Salad

(Serves 4–6 persons)

For variety, add chopped boiled egg in between.

Ingredients

For the dressing:
- Mix together   cup mayonnaise
-   cup fat-free yoghurt
-   cup parsley, chopped
- ½ tsp pepper
- 2 tsp Worcestershire sauce
- 1 tsp garlic, chopped fine
- 1 tsp sugar

For the salad:
- 3 cups cabbage, shredded
- 2 cups broccoli stems, grated
- 2 cups carrots, grated
- 1 cup celery, grated
- 2 cups cauliflower, cut small
-   cup bacon, cooked

Method

In a glass bowl, layer cabbage and broccoli, then spread   of dressing over layered vegetables. Continue to layer carrot, celery and cauliflower and spread remaining dressing over cauliflower. Refrigerate for two hours and sprinkle with bacon. Serve.

200 calories

Warm Potato Salad

(Serves 4 persons)

Eat this as it says – warm.

Ingredients
- 200 gm potatoes, scrubbed and cut into bite-size pieces
- 1 tbsp olive oil
- 1 rasher of bacon, chopped
- 1 tbsp vinegar
- 2 tsp clear honey
- 4 oz spinach leaves, washed
- Salt and freshly ground black pepper to taste

Method
Place potatoes in a pan of lightly salted boiling water. Cover and simmer till tender. Drain and cool. Heat the oil in a frying pan and fry the bacon till crispy. Add the potatoes and fry for another 2 minutes, then add vinegar, honey and seasoning and cook for another minute. Allow a little cooling before arranging on the spinach leaves and serve immediately.

221 calories

Party Stuffed Mushrooms

(Serves 4 persons)

Are mushrooms in season? Try this and have a feast!

Ingredients

- 12 large or 20 small mushrooms
- 1 tsp olive oil
- 1 cup onion, finely chopped
- 1 clove garlic, chopped
- 2 cups fresh spinach, chopped
- 1 tbsp chopped walnuts
- 2 tbsp cheese, grated
- ½ cup breadcrumbs
- Salt and pepper to taste
- 2 tbsp finely chopped parsley (optional)

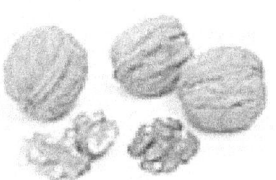

Method

Clean mushrooms with a dry cloth and remove stems. Chop stems finely and set aside with the whole mushroom caps. Heat oil in a large heavy skillet. Sauté onions for 10 to 15 minutes until very soft, adding chopped mushroom stems for the last 5 minutes. Add garlic and cook another minute. Stir in the spinach, nuts, cheese, breadcrumbs, salt and pepper. Cook until spinach wilts. Stuff with the filling and bake at 350 F for 15 minutes or until mushrooms are soft and the tops light brown. Scatter cheese and parsley over the top and serve.

114 calories

Cool Cucumber Salad

(Serves 4 persons)

Eat this and feel as cool as a cucumber!

Ingredients

- 2 medium cucumbers
- 1 tbsp mint leaves, chopped
- 1 tbsp coriander leaves
- ½ cup spring onions, chopped
- Salt and pepper to taste
- ½ cup low-fat yoghurt
- ½ tbsp lemon juice
- ½ tsp ground cumin
- ½ tsp coriander powder

Method

Wash the cucumber and partially peel in long strips, leaving alternating strips of green skin and white flesh. Cut lengthwise into long thin slices, then across into matchsticks. Combine with green onion, coriander leaves and mint in a large bowl. Whisk yoghurt, lime juice, cumin, coriander, salt and pepper. Toss with the vegetables and marinate for 10 minutes. Serve with any spicy dish.

38 calories

Low-fat Ranch Dressing with Herbs

(Serves 4 persons)

If you want a dressing that is thick and economical, you need to try this. It fits the bill perfectly!

Ingredients
- cup well-shaken low-fat buttermilk
- 2 tbsp low-fat mayonnaise
- 2 tbsp non-fat sour cream
- 1 tbsp packed fresh coriander leaves, minced
- 2 tsp vinegar
- 1 tsp dry mustard
- 1 garlic clove, minced
- ½ tsp sugar

Method
Blend all ingredients in a blender or food processor until smooth. Add salt and pepper to taste. Covered and chilled, dressing keeps for one week. Serve with any salad or soft lettuce. Makes about one cup.

One tbsp = 12 calories (approx.)

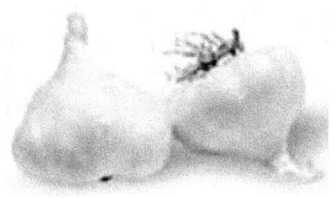

Eggplant with Roasted Peanuts

(Serves 4 persons)

Try this dish for a change and see how versatile eggplant (brinjal) is.

Ingredients
- 1½ tbsp fish sauce
- 4 tsp sugar
- 2 tsp fresh lime juice
- ½ kg long thin eggplants
- 1 tsp vegetable oil
- kg long beans or other green beans
- 10 tomatoes
- 2 tbsp fresh coriander leaves
- 1 tbsp roasted peanuts

Method

Stir together fish sauce, sugar, and lime juice and let stand for about 10 minutes, stirring occasionally, until sugar is dissolved. Preheat broiler. Cut eggplants crosswise into half-inch-thick slices. Brush a small baking pan with some oil and place eggplant slices in pan. Brush eggplant with remaining oil and broil 3 to 4 inches from heat (turning it once) until tender and browned, for about 8 minutes. Combine eggplant with fish-sauce mixture and toss.

Prepare a bowl of ice and cold water. Cut beans into 1½-inch length and cook in a saucepan of boiling salted water for two minutes. Drain beans and place into ice water to stop cooking. Drain beans well and mix with eggplant mixture. Cut tomatoes in half and coarsely chop coriander leaves. Finely chop peanuts. Mix tomatoes, coriander leaves and some peanuts into eggplant mixture, tossing to combine. Vegetables may be prepared two hours ahead. Serve vegetables at room temperature sprinkled with remaining peanuts.

74 calories per serving

Baked Corn on the Cob

(Serves 4 persons)

If you want this spicier, add chilli powder too.

Ingredients
- 4 corn cobs, husks and silk removed
- 4 tbsp water
- 50 gm butter, melted
- Sugar
- Few pieces of aluminium foil

Method
Place each corn on a piece of foil large enough to contain it and sprinkle with a little sugar, salt and a tablespoon of water. Seal the edges of the foil firmly to make parcels. Grill for 10 to 15 minutes till tender.

Open the parcels and pour over melted butter. Serve straight from the foil.

223 calories per serving

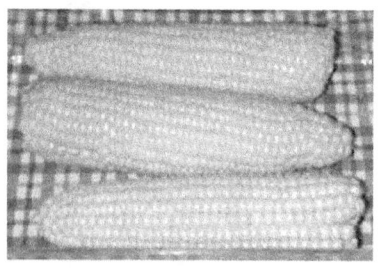

Potatoes Lyonnaise

(Serves 4–6 persons)

Serve this as an occasional treat... because of the calories!

Ingredients
- 1 kg potatoes
- 2 large onions
- 25 gm butter
- 1 tbsp cooking oil
- Salt and pepper to taste
- Coriander leaves, chopped

Method
Peel the potatoes and cook in boiling salted water till tender. Drain and allow cooling. Cut into thick slices. Peel and thinly slice onions. Melt the butter and oil together in a large frying pan, add the onions and fry for three minutes till they become transparent. Add the potatoes, seasoning and leaves and stir well. Divide the mixture in half and place each onto large squares of double thickness foil. Bring the edges up together and seal tightly leaving room for the expansion of steam. Bake for half an hour until potatoes are tender when pierced.

570–650 calories

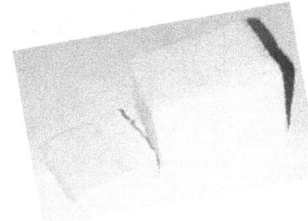

Tomato and Onion Grill

(Serves 2–4 persons)

Are you feeling hungry and looking to simply hog? Binge on this and stay low on calories!

Ingredients
- 3 large tomatoes
- 2 large onions
- 2 tbsp olive oil
- Few mint leaves

Method
Slice the tomatoes and onions thickly. Lay them alternately on a sheet of aluminium foil. Sprinkle oil, salt and pepper and the mint leaves over the vegetables. Grill for 3 to 6 minutes till tender.

58 calories

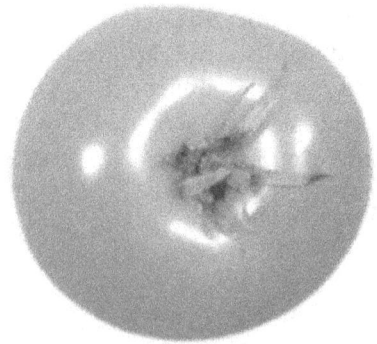

Cucumber and Celery Filling

(Serves 4 persons)

Have some bread on hand? Spread it with this.

Ingredients
- 100 gm butter
- 3-inch piece cucumber, peeled and finely chopped
- 1 large celery stalk, finely chopped
- Salt and pepper

Method
Beat together the butter, cucumber and celery. Add salt and pepper to taste and mix well.

286 calories

Stuffed Mushrooms

(Serves 4 persons)

Fry bacon crisply and sprinkle on the grilled mushrooms and voila – you have a delicious treat!

Ingredients
- 8 large mushrooms
- 2 tbsp breadcrumbs
- 1 onion, chopped
- 1 tomato, skinned and chopped
- 1 tsp coriander leaves
- 1 tbsp oil

Method
Remove the stalks from the mushrooms and chop them finely. Mix the stalks with breadcrumbs, onion, leaves and tomato. Brush the mushroom caps with oil and arrange on an oiled ovenproof plate. Spread each cap with the stuffing and grill to cook. Serve decorated with mint leaves.

48 calories

Yummy Stuffed Potatoes

(Serves 4 persons)

With this recipe, turn ordinary potatoes into a chef's delight!

Ingredients

- 4 large potatoes
- 100 gm soft cheese
- 1 onion, chopped
- 1 tbsp coriander leaves
- Salt and pepper to taste

Method

Parboil potatoes for a few minutes. Prick all over with a fork and rub with salt. Wrap each potato in foil and bake for about half an hour or more till potatoes are soft. Keep turning frequently. Meanwhile, cream together the cheese, onions, leaves and seasoning. Scoop the flesh from the cooked potatoes and mix in the cheese mixture. Arrange back into the potato shells and serve.

280 calories

Potato Cheese Hash

(Serves 4–6 persons)

This is so simple and good to serve with roast meat.

Ingredients
- 1 kg potatoes, cleaned and cut into cubes
- 200 gm cheese
- 1 onion, chopped
- Salt and pepper

Method
Parboil the potato cubes in salted water for about 3 minutes. Drain well. Chop the cheese into 1-cm cubes as well. Cut four square pieces of foil. Divide the potato, cheese and onion between the pieces of foil and season with salt and pepper. Make foil parcels ensuring the edges are secured tightly. Bake the packets for 30 minutes or so till tender when pierced with a skewer.

250 calories

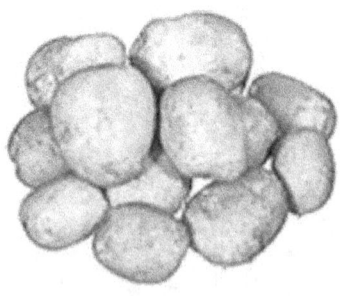

Brazilian Salad

(Serves 4 persons)

Enjoy the flavours of Brazil without even leaving your home!

Ingredients

For French dressing:

- Mix 2 tbsp vinegar with 6–8 tbsp olive oil, salt and pepper
- 4 tbsp French dressing
- 3 bananas, peeled and thinly sliced
- 1 tbsp lemon juice
- 100 gm nuts, chopped (walnuts or peanuts)
- 1 crisp head of lettuce leaves

Method

Arrange half the lettuce leaves in a shallow salad bowl. Shred the rest of the lettuce into a mixing bowl and pour the French dressing over it. Mix the bananas and the nuts and add to the shredded lettuce. Pile the nuts and banana mixture on top of the lettuce leaves in the serving bowl. Arrange some banana slices around the salad.

396 calories

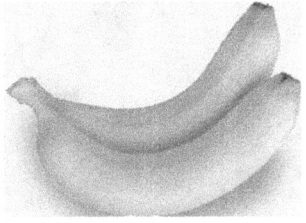

Mushroom and Cheese Salad

(Serves 4 persons)

Enjoy this salad with your loved ones.

Ingredients

- 200 gm cheese cut into cubes
- 100 gm button mushrooms, quartered
- 1 tbsp coriander leaves
- 4 large lettuce leaves

For the dressing, mix together:

- 6 tbsp olive oil
- 2 tbsp vinegar
- 2 garlic cloves, crushed
- Salt and freshly ground pepper

Method

Place the mushrooms and cheese in a bowl. Add the dressing and toss well. Leave aside for half an hour. Line a salad bowl with lettuce leaves. Spoon the cheese mixture over on top of the lettuce and sprinkle with chopped leaves.

423 calories

Simple Potato Salad

(Serves 4–6 persons)

Serve this with hamburgers or steaks garnished with chopped spring onions.

Ingredients
- ½ kg potatoes
- 2 tsp olive oil
- 2 tsp vinegar
- 4 tbsp soured cream
- 1 tbsp spring onions, chopped
- Salt and pepper to taste

Method
Cook the potatoes in boiling salted water for 15 to 20 minutes till tender. Drain and cut into half-inch pieces. Place in a bowl. While still warm, add the oil and vinegar to the potatoes. Leave to cool. Whisk the soured cream, then carefully mix it into the potatoes with a wooden spoon. Season with salt and pepper and sprinkle leaves before serving.

131 calories

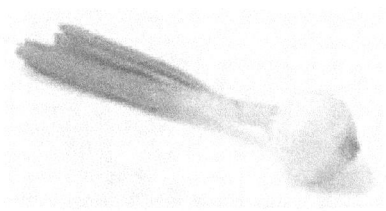

Simple Relish

(Serves 4 persons)

This can be stored for about three days in the refrigerator.

Ingredients
- 1 can of sweet corn
- 4 tbsp vinegar
- 2 tbsp oil
- 1 tsp sugar
- 2 sticks celery, diced
- Half a cucumber, diced
- Salt to taste

Method
Drain the sweet corn and mix the sweet corn and cucumber. Add all the remaining ingredients.

Refrigerate for about two hours and serve with meat.

124 calories

Easy Mint Chutney

(Serves 2 persons)

Enjoy this with chapattis.

Ingredients
- 2 tbsp fresh mint, chopped
- 2 spring onions, chopped
- 1 tsp sugar
- 1 small green chilli, deseeded and chopped
- 1 tbsp lemon juice
- Pinch of garam masala
- 2 tbsp yoghurt

Method
Place all these ingredients in a blender and puree well. Add more salt and sugar if needed.

14 calories

Meat and Poultry Dishes

Cheese Chicken Drumsticks

(Serves 4 persons)

Cut the calories with this grilled chicken.

Ingredients
- 4 large chicken drumsticks, skinned
- 2 oz fresh breadcrumbs
- 2 oz cheese, grated
- 1 tbsp plain flour
- 1 egg, beaten
- Salt and pepper to taste

Method

Mix the breadcrumbs and cheese. Season the flour with salt and pepper. Coat the drumsticks with flour and dip in the beaten egg. Then roll in the breadcrumb mixture and press it well. Make sure the pieces are well coated. Chill in the refrigerator for about half an hour. Grill the drumsticks for about 30 minutes or till cooked, turning frequently until tender. Serve immediately.

138 calories

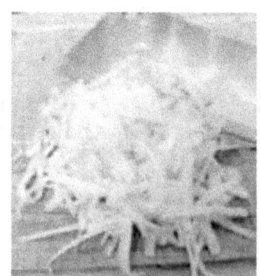

Simple Bread Pizza

(Serves 4–6 persons)

Try this simple pizza that's different!

Ingredients
- 6 to 8 slices of bread
- 1 tsp olive oil
- 200 gm tomatoes, chopped
- 1 oz ham, thinly sliced
- Pinch of dried chilli flakes
- 2 cloves garlic, chopped
- 1 oz low-fat cheese
- Coriander leaves
- 1 egg
- Salt and pepper to taste

Method

Preheat oven. Drizzle the oil on the bread and bake for about 5 to 10 minutes. Mix tomatoes, ham, chilli, garlic, salt and round black pepper together.

Remove the bread base from the oven and top with this mixture, cheese and leaves. Make a slight hollow in the centre of the topping and carefully crack the egg on top of the pizza and bake for 10 to 15 minutes till cooked. Serve with fresh green salad.

409 calories

Sunset Stir-fry

(Serves 4–6 persons)

Enjoy the sunset with this stir-fry by the beach!

Ingredients
- 450 gm chicken meat
- 1 tbsp soya sauce
- 1 tbsp vegetable oil
- 1 onion chopped
- 1 cucumber, sliced diagonally
- 1 green pepper, deseeded and cut into strips
- 2 oz mushrooms, sliced
- 1 oz bean sprouts
- 4 oz broccoli, cut into florets
- 1 oz cashew-nuts
- 2 oz baby corn (optional)

Method
In a bowl, marinate the chicken pieces with soya sauce, salt and pepper. In a wok, heat oil, add the chicken pieces and fry till browned. Add the prepared vegetables and nuts and stir-fry at high heat for about 6 minutes making sure the vegetables are crisp but tender. Serve hot with a bowl of plain white rice and watch it disappear!

200 calories

Honey Mustard Chicken

(Serves 5 persons)

This is a delicious chicken fun meal. You can marinate and freeze this and have fun later!

Ingredients

- 10 good chicken pieces, skin removed
- ½ cup mustard
- ½ cup honey
- 2 tbsp chopped coriander leaves
- 1 tsp grated orange peel

Method

Preheat oven to 400 F. Combine mustard and honey in small bowl. Stir in grated orange peel and leaves. Refrigerate until ready to use. If making only a few pieces, refrigerate in airtight container and use when ready. Line the baking sheet with foil. Place chicken on sheet and coat both sides with mixture. Bake for 30 minutes or until no longer pink inside.

115 calories

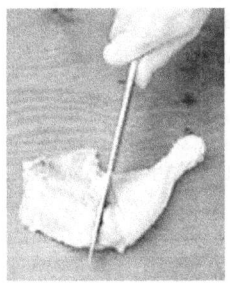

Chicken Drumsticks

(Serves 4 persons)

This marinade is a little different.

Ingredients

- 1 tbsp oil
- 1 large onion, chopped
- 1 clove garlic, crushed
- 3 tbsp vinegar
- 2 tbsp Worcestershire sauce
- Dash of Tabasco sauce
- 2 tbsp tomato puree
- 1 chicken stock cube dissolved in 6 tbsp boiling water
- 1 tbsp brown sugar
- 8 chicken drumsticks

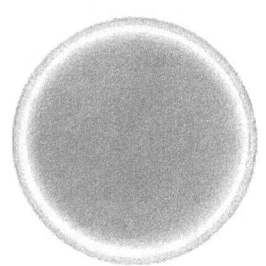

Method

Heat oil in pan and fry onion and garlic until onion is soft. Add the remaining sauce ingredients and simmer gently for three minutes. Divide into two. Heat oven to 180 C/350 F. Place chicken drumsticks in a roasting tin. Baste the drumsticks frequently with one half of the mixture. Cook for about 30 minutes until the juices run clear when the drumstick is pricked with a knife. Baste frequently throughout the cooking.

Use remaining mixture as a sauce to serve with chicken.

199 calories

Roast Lemon Chicken

(Serves 6 persons)

Enjoy this sumptuous chicken straight from the pan!

Ingredients
- 6 boneless chicken breasts with skin
- 1 onion cut into 8 wedges
- 500 gm potatoes washed and cut into wedges
- Juice of 1 large lemon
- 2 tsp honey
- 1½ tbsp olive oil
- 6 cloves garlic, crushed
- Salt and pepper to taste
- Mint and coriander leaves

Method
Preheat oven. In a non-stick pan, dry-fry the chicken till well browned. Place the chicken, onion and potato in a large roasting pan. Mix the lemon juice, olive oil, honey, garlic, salt, pepper and chopped leaves and pour over the chicken in the pan. Bake in the preheated oven till chicken is well cooked and potatoes are tender. Serve immediately from roasting pan.

307 calories per serving

Chicken, Mushroom and Pineapple Salad

(Serves 4 persons)

Try this rice salad for a refreshing change!

Ingredients
- 100 gm basmati rice, cooked and well drained
- 12 oz cold cooked chicken meat, thickly sliced
- 2 tbsp coriander leaves
- 300 gm button mushrooms
- 1 green pepper, deseeded and cut into thin strips
- 200 gm pineapple, cut into small pieces and drained

Dressing ingredients:
- 2 tbsp sesame oil
- 2 tbsp vinegar
- Salt and pepper to taste

Method
Whisk all the dressing ingredients and keep aside till rice cools. In a bowl, mix the rice gently with the salad ingredients. Add the dressing and toss lightly till well coated. Serve.

310 calories per serving

Chicken Kebabs

(Serves 4 persons)

Try these healthy chicken kebabs and feel light all day!

Ingredients

- 4 chicken fillets (about 400 gm)
- 200 gm non-fat yoghurt
- 2 tsp turmeric
- 2 tsp ginger, ground
- 2 cloves garlic, crushed
- 1 tsp cinnamon, powdered
- 4 cloves, crushed
- 1 small pineapple, cut into chunks

Method

Cut the chicken into bite-sized pieces. Mix together all other ingredients except the pineapple. Add chicken pieces and coat well. Thread chicken and pineapple alternately on coconut leaf sticks. Brush with marinade and grill or cook on barbecue till cooked. Serve with Rice Combination Salad (*recipe given on page 39*).

200 calories

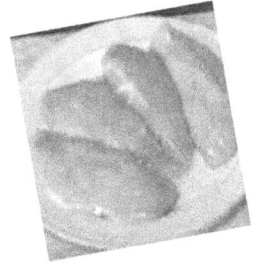

Barbecued Chicken

(Serves 5 persons)

This is an unbelievably easy recipe that you will surely make over and over again.

Ingredients

- 10 chicken drumsticks
- 4 tbsp tomato ketchup
- 1 tbsp vinegar
- 4 tbsp honey
- Salt and pepper to taste
- 4 cloves garlic, smashed

Method

Mix the ketchup, vinegar, honey, garlic, salt and pepper in a bowl. Brush each drumstick with the glaze. Grill in hot oven for about 15 to 20 minutes till cooked. Turn the chicken frequently and brush with the glaze. Serve with hot garlic bread and enjoy.

250 calories

Honey Chicken

(Serves 4 persons)

Cook the sauce and use as a marinade. Yummmm!

Ingredients
- 4 chicken drumsticks, scored
- 1 onion, finely chopped
- 400 gm tomatoes, mashed
- 2 tbsp Worcestershire sauce
- 1 tbsp honey
- 100 gm mushrooms to garnish
- Coriander leaves to garnish

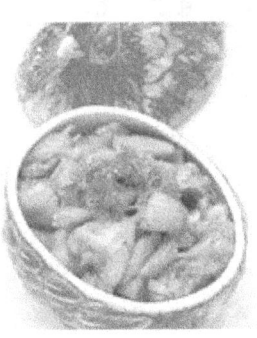

Method
Put the onion, tomatoes, sauce, honey, salt and pepper in a saucepan and cook for about 10 minutes, stirring occasionally. Place the drumsticks on the grill pan and spread with the cooked sauce and cook for about 10 to 15 minutes on each side till cooked, basting with the sauce. Halfway through cooking time, put the mushrooms around the chicken. Brush with the sauce and grill until cooked.

Serve this delicious chicken on a bed of white rice, garnished with mushrooms and coriander leaves and remaining sauce.

230 calories

Chicken Soufflé

(Serves 4–6 persons)

This is an unusual soufflé. Try it and you will see why.

Ingredients
- 2 cups chicken breast strips, cooked and cubed
- 1½ cups long-grain white rice, cooked
- 3 whole hard-boiled eggs, chopped
- ½ cup onions, chopped
- cup low-fat mayonnaise
- 1 cup cream of mushroom soup
- ½ cup cornflakes, powdered
- tsp salt

Method
Preheat oven. Butter a casserole dish. Combine the rice, chicken, eggs, onions and salt in a mixing bowl. Mix well. Fold in the soup and mayonnaise. Mix well. Spoon and spread mixture evenly into prepared dish. Sprinkle cornflakes over the top and bake for about half an hour.

228 calories

Orange Glazed Chicken Tenders

(Serves 4 persons)

Orange and chicken is a good combination and this dish is no exception.

Ingredients

- 2 tsp olive oil
- ½ kg chicken pieces
- Salt and ground black pepper to taste
- ⅓ cup orange marmalade
- 2 tbsp vinegar
- 1 tbsp peeled and ground fresh ginger
- 1 small orange cut into wedges
- 1 tbsp coriander leaves

Method

Heat oil in a non-stick skillet until hot. Place chicken pieces in skillet and sprinkle with salt and pepper. Cook until they are slightly browned on the outside and have lost the pink colour on the inside. This will take about 4 minutes on each side. While the chicken is cooking, mix marmalade, vinegar and ginger in a small bowl. Add this mixture to the skillet containing the chicken, then heat to a boil. Upon reaching boiling point your delicious entrée is ready for garnish. Garnish with the orange wedges and parsley to serve.

220 calories

Lamb Meatballs

(Serves 4–6 persons)

Use very tender meat for this dish.

Ingredients
- 50 gm sultanas (*kismis*)
- 700 gm minced meat
- 8 oz fresh breadcrumbs
- 2 eggs, beaten
- 2 tbsp curry powder
- Salt and pepper
- 2 onions, sliced into rings

Method
Soak the sultanas in water for about an hour. Drain. In a mixing bowl, mix the minced meat with breadcrumbs, sultanas, eggs, curry powder and the seasoning. Mix together and shape into meatballs. Arrange the meatballs onto skewers along with the onion rings.

Grill for 20 minutes or more till cooked. Serve with hot white rice.

392 calories

Caribbean Chicken

(Serves 6 persons)

Make sure the chicken is scored before marinating.

Ingredients
- 6 chicken legs
- 1 tbsp soya sauce
- 100 gm chopped pineapple with juice
- 6 tbsp oil
- 1 clove garlic, chopped

Method
Mix all the ingredients with the chicken. Leave to marinate for two hours or more. Season with salt and pepper and grill till cooked. Keep turning the chicken frequently so that it is basted with the sauce. Cook and serve.

279 calories

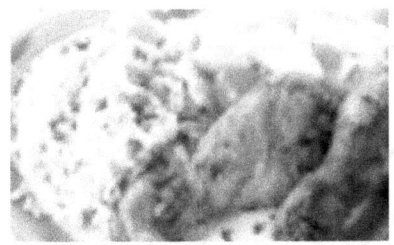

Seafood Dishes

Salmon Mousse

(Serves 4 persons)

If salmon is unavailable, substitute with some other fish or chicken.

Ingredients
- ½ cup hot water
- 3 tsp gelatine
- 220 gm salmon
- 4 shallots, chopped
- cup mayonnaise
- 2 tsp lemon juice
- ½ cup non-fat yoghurt
- Freshly ground pepper
- Lettuce leaves (optional)

Method
Put hot water and gelatine in a blender and blend on high speed for a minute. Add salmon, shallots, mayonnaise, lemon juice and pepper and blend for a further minute. Add yoghurt and blend for 30 seconds. Pour salmon mixture into small individual bowls or one large bowl and refrigerate until set and serve on lettuce leaf with toast triangles.

635 calories

Simple Salmon

(Serves 4 persons)

You have heard of Simple Simon, haven't you? Bet you haven't heard of Simple Salmon!

Ingredients

- 4 salmon steaks
- 4 tbsp sunflower oil
- 6 sprigs of mint or coriander leaves
- 2 lemons
- ½ cucumber, sliced
- Salt and pepper to taste

Method

Lay the salmon steaks in a shallow dish and pour the oil over them. Sprinkle the leaves, salt and pepper. Cut the lemon in half. Squeeze the juice of one lemon over the salmon steaks and cut the other one into slices. Marinate the salmon for about half an hour and grill for a few minutes on each side till the flesh has turned pink and is firm. Serve on a bed of sliced cucumber with the lemon slices.

302 calories

Tuna Pate

(Serves 4–6 persons)

This is good with toast.

Ingredients
- 4 oz butter
- 2 garlic cloves, crushed
- 400 gm tuna, cooked with salt and pepper
- 2 tbsp olive oil
- 1 tbsp lemon juice
- Coriander leaves, chopped

Method
Mix the butter with garlic. Cut the tuna into pieces. Blend half the tuna with half the melted butter mixture and half the olive oil, in a food processor or blender. Blend till smooth. Remove and do the same with the rest of the fish and butter mixture. Mix in the lemon juice. Spoon into a serving dish. Chill and serve with toast.

159 calories

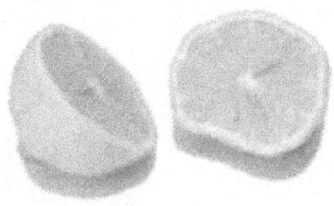

Honey Sardines

(Serves 4–6 persons)

This dish is light, yet tasty and satisfying.

Ingredients
- 12 fresh sardines
- 2 tbsp lemon juice
- 2 tbsp vinegar
- 1 tbsp clear honey
- 1 tbsp oil

Method
Place sardines in a shallow dish. Make the marinade by beating the lemon juice with the vinegar, honey, and oil. Blend it well. Pour over the sardines, cover and leave to marinate in the refrigerator for 2 to 3 hours, turning occasionally. Remove the sardines with a slotted spoon and place on the wire mesh under the grill and cook for 8 to 10 minutes till cooked. Baste with marinade in between. Serve hot with chive butter (*see below for this recipe*).

600 calories

Chive butter:

Beat together 50 gm butter with 1 tsp lemon juice, 1 tsp coriander leaves, salt and pepper.

Surprise Fish Parcels

(Serves 4 persons)

Like surprises? Treat yourself to this one.

Ingredients
- 4 fish steaks
- 8 button mushrooms
- 1 onion, peeled and chopped
- 4 tomatoes
- 2 oz peas
- 1 oz butter
- 1 tbsp lemon juice

Method
Place each fish steak on a square of foil. Sprinkle with salt and pepper. Slice the mushrooms and chop the tomatoes. Divide the mushrooms, peas, onions and tomatoes over the fish steaks. Dot with butter, then sprinkle with lemon juice. Wrap the foil loosely around the fish, making sure the folds are tightly sealed.

Place under the grill and cook for about half an hour till the fish is cooked. Serve sprinkled with chopped coriander leaves.

148 calories

Baked Whole Fish with Vegetable Stuffing

(Serves 6–8 persons)

This is a good treat to serve your family. The only problem is you might not have any leftovers!

Ingredients
- 1½ kg fish, cleaned and washed
- ½ cup lemon juice
- ½ cup water
- 2 tomatoes, sliced
- 2 onions, sliced
- 2 tbsp coriander leaves
- Salt and freshly ground pepper to taste
- Lemon wedges

Method
Pat fish dry with kitchen paper. Place whole fish in a lightly oiled baking dish and sprinkle with pepper. Mix little salt with lemon juice and water. Pour this mixture over fish and bake for about 20 to 30 minutes. Baste occasionally. Arrange tomato and onion slices alternatively on top of fish. Cover and bake a further 10 to 20 minutes or until fish flakes easily with a fork along backbone. Sprinkle with chopped coriander leaves and serve with sweet potatoes, steamed vegetables and lemon wedges.

140 calories per serving

To serve fish with julienne stuffing:

Ingredients
- 1 carrot
- 1 capsicum
- 2 sweet potatoes (you can add any vegetable)
- 2–3 tsp margarine
- 1 tsp coriander powder
- Salt and pepper to taste

Method
Cut the vegetables in fine matchsticks. Heat margarine and toss vegetables in the margarine with seasonings. Use this stuffing for the whole fish and enjoy. (This stuffing can also be used in whole chicken.)

120 calories

Fish Turbans

(Serves 4–6 persons)

Enjoy eating like a king? Then try this and feel like one!

Ingredients

- 1 carrot and 2 sticks celery, cut into thin strips
- ½ kg (4–6 pieces) white fish fillets
- 1 chicken stock cube mixed with a cup of water
- 2 tbsp lemon juice
- 2 tsp corn flour mixed in 2 tbsp extra water
- 2 tbsp chopped coriander leaves

Method

Boil, steam or microwave the carrot and celery till tender. Wrap each fish fillet around a little of the vegetables. Combine stock cube mixture and juice in frying pan and bring to boil. Add fish turbans, cover and cook over low heat for about 5 to 7 minutes till cooked. Remove fish from stock and keep warm.

Blend corn flour with extra water and bring to boil stirring till sauce is thickened. Stir in the coriander leaves and serve sauce over fish.

286 calories per serving

Fish Bean Steak

(Serves 1 person)

Feel like having a meal by yourself? Try this – it serves one.

Ingredients
- 1 cup beans, cut into uniform length
- 1 large tomato, sliced
- 1 piece fish fillet of 4 oz
- 1 egg, boiled
- 1 tsp olive oil
- 1 tsp vinegar

Method
Season the fish. Heat cook fish in non-stick pan with oil. Mix the tomato, beans and vinegar together. Slice the egg thickly. In a serving plate, decorate cooked fish with the tomato mixture and the egg and serve.

290 calories per serving

Asian Stir-fry

(Serves 2–4 persons)

Try this stir-fry on a bed of steamed white rice – it's delicious!

Ingredients

- ½ kg shrimp
- 3 large garlic cloves, minced
-    cup onion, sliced
- Salt and pepper to taste
- 1 tbsp oil
- ½ cup fresh green peas, cooked
- 1 cup green pepper, chopped
- 1 cup carrots, chopped
- 1 cup broccoli, chopped
- 2 tbsp vegetable broth
- 1 tbsp lemon juice

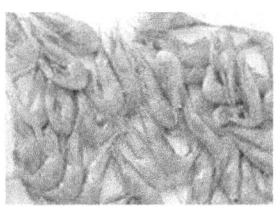

Method

Place drained shrimp in a bowl. Add salt and pepper to shrimp. Toss well. Heat oil in a wok on high. Sauté shrimp stirring frequently for about 5 minutes. Place sautéed shrimp back into the bowl leaving the liquids in the wok. Combine the onions and garlic in the wok and sauté for about 3 minutes. Add peas, vegetables and broth to the wok. Reduce heat to medium and cook for about 4 minutes until vegetables are crisp and tender. Return shrimp to wok, add lemon juice and cook for an extra minute.

153 calories

Oriental Fish

(Serves 4 persons)

Go Chinese with this dish!

Ingredients
- 6 tbsp soy sauce
- 2 garlic cloves, crushed
- 2 tbsp sesame oil
- 2 tbsp brown sugar
- 2 tbsp lemon juice
- 2 tsp ginger, crushed
- 4 fish, whole or thin medium slices
- 2 spring onions, chopped

Method
Mix soy sauce, garlic, oil, sugar, lemon juice and ginger together and pour into a shallow dish. Lay the fish on top and keep turning fish in marinade a couple of times. Leave for an hour. Cover the grill with greased foil and place fish on top. Grill for a few minutes till cooked. Sprinkle with the spring onion and serve with lemon wedges.

166 calories

Mustard Tuna

(Serves 4 persons)

A meal by itself, tuna steaks can be marinated and stored in the freezer till needed.

Ingredients
- 2 oz or 50 gm butter
- 3 tsp mustard
- 2 tbsp lemon juice
- 4 individual tuna steaks
- Lemon slices for garnish
- Salt and pepper

Method
Combine the melted butter with the mustard, lemon juice and seasoning to taste. Brush half the mixture over the fish on both sides, then grill for about 10 to 12 minutes till cooked. Turn brush with the remaining mixture and grill till cooked. Serve hot with remaining mustard mixture, if any and lemon slices to garnish. Serve with salad and hot noodles.

207 calories

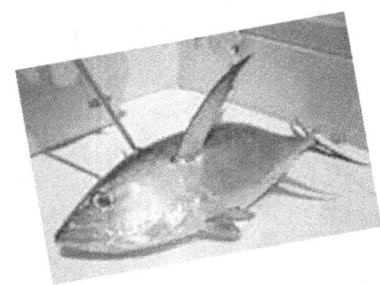

Barbecued Fish with Mushroom Stuffing

(Serves 4 persons)

Explore the underworld with this barbecued fish!

Ingredients
- 350 gm mushrooms
- 2 shallots, thinly sliced
- Juice of 2 limes
- 1 lime cut into quarters
- 4 white fish pieces, cleaned and scored diagonally
- Mixed salad leaves

Method
Divide the fish into two without cutting through to completely divide. Mix together the mushrooms, shallots and lime juice. Use half this mixture to stuff the fish and keep the remainder for the side salad. Put the fish in wrap in lightly oiled foil. Sprinkle salt and pepper.

Cook on the barbecue for around 10 to 15 minutes on each side. Toss the leftover mushroom mixture with the mixed salad leaves and serve with the fish and a wedge of lime.

139 calories

Delicious Tuna Filling

(Serves 4 persons)

You can use canned tuna if you wish.

Ingredients
- 8 oz tuna fish, cooked and flaked
- 2 tsp vinegar
- 2 tomatoes, skinned and finely chopped
- 2 tbsp tomato ketchup
- 2 oz soft butter
- Salt and pepper to taste

Method
Mix together tuna fish, tomato ketchup, vinegar and tomatoes. Add the salt and pepper to taste and mix in the butter.

82 calories

Special Stuffed Tomatoes

(Serves 4 persons)

This is not only pretty to look at but tasty as well.

Ingredients
- 200 gm tuna, cooked and flaked
- 1 celery stalk, chopped
- 2 tbsp onion, chopped
- 2 tbsp green pepper
- 2 tbsp mayonnaise
- 4 large tomatoes
- 6 lettuce leaves
- 4 lemon slices to garnish
- Salt and pepper to taste

Method
Mix together the tuna, celery, onion, green pepper, mayonnaise, salt and pepper to taste. With the stem end down, cut each tomato into 6 wedges cutting down to but not through the base. Spread the wedges apart slightly and sprinkle salt. Place the leaves on a serving plate. Put the tomatoes on the lettuce. Spoon equal amounts of the tuna mixture into the centre of each tomato. Garnish with twisted slices of lemon.

69 calories

Chilled Prawns

(Serves 4–6 persons)

This is for when you want to have something extra special or to serve to someone you love!

Ingredients

- 20 jumbo prawns, cooked
- 10 small green chillies, deseeded and cut in half
- 5 tbsp olive oil
- Salt to taste
- Lemon wedges

Method

Preheat oven. Wrap one half of each chilli round the middle of a jumbo prawn and thread five of each onto a skewer (kebab style). Place the skewers in a long shallow dish and cover with the oil and salt.

Leave covered in a cool place for at least half an hour. Cook the prawns on a greased grill of an oven for 3 minutes on each side, basting with any leftover marinade. Serve hot with lemon wedges.

244 calories

Peppered Fish Kebabs

(Serves 4–6 persons)

This is good as part of a barbecue.

Ingredients

- 500 gm fish, cut into one-inch cubes
- 150 ml yoghurt
- 1 tbsp black peppercorns, lightly crushed
- 3 tbsp olive oil
- Salt to taste
- Lemon slices to garnish

Method

Put the fish cubes in a large bowl. Add the yoghurt, peppercorns, oil and slat. Stir everything well and leave for about an hour to marinate. Thread the fish onto long skewers and grill for about 10 to 15 minutes till cooked. Baste with the marinade in between. Serve garnished with lemon slices.

140 calories

Grape and Prawn Fresh Salad

(Serves 4 persons)

Try including melon balls into this salad and feast on the appreciation!

Ingredients

- 350 gm cottage cheese (paneer)
- 100 gm green grapes
- 200 gm prawns, peeled
- 4 tbsp mayonnaise
- 4 tbsp lemon juice
- 3 tbsp coriander leaves
- Lemon slices
- Salt and pepper to taste
- Lettuce leaves

Method

Place lettuce leaves to line the base of the salad bowl. Next, mix the prawns, cheese, grapes, salt and pepper together. Place this mixture over the lettuce leaves. Mix the mayonnaise, lemon juice and leaves together and spoon it over the cottage cheese mixture. Garnish with the lemon slices and serve.

282 calories

Greek Fish Starter

(Serves 6 persons)

This is an ideal starter from Greece for your guests that stirs and shakes their appetites for bigger and better things!

Ingredients

- 1 slice of bread, crust removed
- 2 garlic cloves
- 4 tbsp olive oil
- 8 oz or 225 gm boneless fish, cooked with salt and pepper
- 1 small potato, cooked and peeled
- 2 tsp lemon juice
- 2 tbsp iced water
- Salt and pepper
- Lemon slices to garnish

Method

Soak the bread in cold water. Squeeze dry. In a blender, blend the garlic, potato, fish, oil, lemon juice, bread and coriander leaves one at a time. Add a little of the cold water as needed till a smooth consistency is obtained. Store in the refrigerator covered with cling wrap or foil. Make sure the top is smoothened. Serve garnished with lemon wedges.

This can be used as a dip with salted biscuits or dry toast.

167 calories

Barbecued Fish

(Serves 4 persons)

Remember to use only fish that is fresh and firm for this recipe and watch it become a favourite among weight watchers!

Ingredients

- 2 oz or 50 gm butter
- 3 tbsp lemon juice
- 3 tbsp coriander leaves
- Salt and pepper to taste
- 4 fish, kept whole, cleaned, washed and scored
- Lemon slices to garnish

Method

Mix together the lemon juice, butter, leaves, salt and pepper. Brush the fish with this mixture all over. Cook on the grill or barbecue, turning several times with the marinade. Turn the fish carefully. If you wish, you can place the fish on foil and cook. Enjoy!

300 calories

Desserts

Nutty Peaches

(Serves 4 persons)

This is a lovely, sweet and savoury dish.

Ingredients
- 4 ripe peaches
- 2 tbsp lemon juice
- 225 gm cottage cheese (paneer)
- 100 gm nuts, chopped
- 8 lettuce leaves

Method
Place the peaches in a mixing bowl and sprinkle with lemon juice. Toss well. Meanwhile, mix the cottage cheese and nuts together. Arrange the leaves decoratively on four individual serving dishes. Place two peach halves on each dish, cut sides up. Spoon the cottage cheese mixture into the centres. Serve garnished with a mint leaf on top.

292 calories

Apple Delight with Custard Sauce

(Serves 4–6 persons)

Have a sweet tooth and don't know what to do about it? Eat this delight and satisfy your sweet tooth without bother!

Ingredients

- cup wheat flour mixed with 1 tsp baking powder
- cup plain flour mixed with   tsp baking powder
- 2 tbsp margarine
- 2 tbsp water
- Little jam, as needed
- 2 apples, grated
- 1 cup apple juice
- ½ tsp cinnamon, powdered

Method

Sift the flours in a bowl. Rub in the margarine until the mixture resembles breadcrumbs. Add water and mix into a dough. Knead lightly on a floured board and roll out thinly into an oblong shape. Spread with the jam as needed and spread the grated apple evenly over the dough. Roll up and place in a lightly oiled ovenproof dish. Heat the apple juice and pour over the fruit roll carefully. Sprinkle with cinnamon and score the pastry diagonally with a knife. Bake uncovered in a moderately hot oven for about 20 minutes till golden. Serve with custard sauce (*recipe given on next page*).

185 calories per serving

To make Custard Sauce:

Ingredients
- 3 tbsp custard powder
- 1 tbsp sugar
- 4 tbsp skim milk powder
- 2 cups hot water
- 2 tsp vanilla essence

Method
Combine custard powder, sugar and milk powder in a saucepan. Gradually blend in the water and bring to a boil till the mixture thickens. Flavour with vanilla and serve with the apple delight. It is a healthy delight indeed!

360 calories

Luscious Strawberry Whip

(Serves 4 persons)

Have strawberries? Make this and savour each and every bite!

Ingredients
- 250 gm strawberries
- cup sugar
- cup orange juice
- 2 tsp gelatine
- 1 tbsp water
- 1 egg white

Method
Reserve 4 strawberries for decoration and blend remaining strawberries with the sugar and juice till smooth. Sprinkle the gelatine over water in a small bowl placed in a pan of simmering water. Stir till dissolved and combine this with the strawberry mixture. Cool until the mixture begins to set. In a small bowl, beat egg white till soft peaks form. Lightly fold beaten egg white into strawberry mixture. Spoon into four serving glasses, then cover and refrigerate for several hours. Decorate each of the glasses with the reserved strawberries.

92 calories

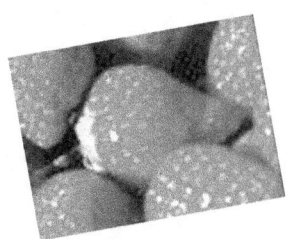

Baked Pineapple

(Serves 4 persons)

This is probably the easiest dessert ever! Talk about saving time!

Ingredients
- 1 ripe pineapple
- 75 gm soft brown sugar
- ½ tsp ginger, ground
- 50 gm coconut, grated
- Strawberries or peaches to decorate (optional)

Method
Cut the fresh pineapple into thick rings with the skin on. Place each ring on a separate square of foil and sprinkle with a little brown sugar and pinch of ginger. Top with the coconut. Wrap the foil securely around the slices and seal. Cook under grill for 10 minutes or more. Serve on individual plates garnished with the strawberry.

261 calories

Dreamy Tropical Pineapple and Lychee

(Serves 4–6 persons)

You can also add a couple of ice cubes in this to keep it cool!

Ingredients
- 1 ripe pineapple
- 300 gm lychees, canned or fresh
- Half a watermelon
- 2 tbsp honey
- 1 tbsp lemon juice

Method
Cut the pineapple in half lengthways and scoop out the flesh and cut into bite-sized pieces, discarding the centre core. Drain the lychees if canned and reserve the syrup. Remove the seeds from the watermelon and scoop out the flesh with a melon-baller or rounded spoon. Mix the syrup from the lychees and the honey together. Place the prepared fruits in a bowl and mix in the syrup mixture. Mix and leave aside to allow the flavours to penetrate. Spoon this into the pineapple halves and serve.

90 calories

Easy Spice Biscuits

(Serves 4–6 persons)

This is a biscuit with a difference and a flavour that will stay on your tongue for some time!

Ingredients

- 150 gm plain flour
- 1 tsp cinnamon, powdered
- 100 gm butter
- 50 gm sugar

Method

Sift the flour and spice together. Cream the butter and sugar together until light and fluffy. Mix in the flour mixture and bind together with your hand. Roll out onto a floured board to a thickness of about 5 mm. Then cut out shapes using a shape cutter. Place each piece on a greased baking sheet and prick with a fork. Bake in a preheated oven for about 15 minutes or till cooked.

Leave the biscuits to cool on a wire rack.

83 calories

Banana Muffins

(Serves 4 persons)

Great treat for kids and adults.

Ingredients

- ½ cup sugar
- 1 tsp baking soda
- tsp salt
- cup flour
- cup whole-wheat flour
- cup vegetable oil
- cup skim milk
- 2 medium bananas, mashed (1 cup)
- 1 tsp vanilla
- ⅓ cup raisins (optional)

Method

Preheat oven. Mix together sugar, baking soda, salt and flour in a bowl. Stir well. Add oil, milk, mashed bananas and vanilla; mix just until flour is moistened.

Fold in raisins. Use a non-stick muffin pan and muffin paper or coat the pan with oil or cooking spray. Fill muffin cups two-thirds with batter. Bake 15 to 20 minutes or until golden brown. Remove from pan right away.

280 calories

Low-calorie Banana Delight

(Serves 2–4 persons)

This is unbelievably low in calories but high in taste and that's the best part of this dish.

Ingredients
- 2 bananas, sliced
- 2 tsp grated orange rind
- ½ cup orange juice
-   cup sultanas
- 1 egg white
- 2 tsp castor sugar

Method
Combine bananas, rind juice and sultanas in base of shallow ovenproof dish. Beat the egg white in a small bowl until soft peaks form, gradually adding sugar. Continue beating until the sugar is dissolved. Spread meringue over the banana mixture and bake in a moderate oven for 10 minutes or until the meringue is golden brown.

96 calories per serving

Watermelon Surprise

(Serves 4–6 persons)

This is an unbelievably easy dessert.

Ingredients

- 6 cups watermelon pieces
- 1 onion, cut into thin slices
- ⅓ cup vinegar
- 3 tbsp mint leaves, chopped
- ½ tsp freshly ground pepper

Method

Chill the watermelon before preparing, especially if it is very ripe. Combine all the ingredients gently and serve cold.

57 calories

Light Crème Brulee

(Serves 4 persons)

Try this dessert and don't feel guilty about the calories!

Ingredients
- 1½ tbsp sugar
- 1 tbsp corn flour
- 1½-cup skim milk
- 1 egg yolk
- ½ tsp vanilla essence
- 1 tbsp brown sugar

Method
Combine sugar and corn flour in a medium saucepan and gradually stir in combined milk and yolk. Beat until smooth. Cook over medium heat stirring constantly until mixture boils and thickens. Add essence. Pour mixture either into a medium serving dish or into four serving dishes. Sprinkle with brown sugar and refrigerate until cold.

104 calories per serving

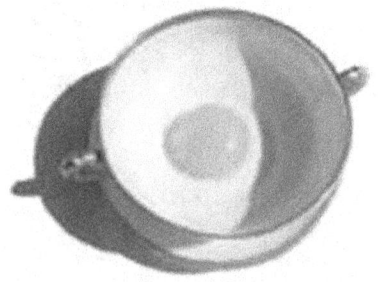

Banana Raisin Muffins

(Serves 4 persons)

Instead of wheat flour, you can proceed with plain white flour.

Ingredients
- ½ cup sugar
- 1 tsp baking soda
- tsp salt
- cup flour
- cup wheat flour
- cup vegetable oil
- cup skim milk
- 1 cup or 2 medium bananas, mashed
- 1 tsp vanilla
- cup raisins (optional)

⅓

Method
Grease muffin cups. Place the flours, sugar, salt and baking powder in a bowl. Add the oil, milk, bananas and vanilla and blend till the mixture is moistened. Fold in the raisins and place batter two-thirds full in each muffin cup. Bake for about 20 minutes till golden brown. Enjoy hot muffins straight from the oven!

250 calories

Pineapple Upside-down Cake

(Serves 6–8 persons)

Serious about cutting sugar from your diet? Then you need to make this cake. But ensure you have plenty of Equal packets around!

Ingredients

- 14 oz pineapple in juice, undrained
- cup nuts, almonds or walnut pieces (optional)
- 2 tbsp lemon juice
- 6 packets Equal sweetener
- 1 tsp cornstarch
- 4 tbsp margarine (at room temperature)
- 12 packets Equal sweetener
- 1 egg
- 1 cup plain flour
- 1½ tsp baking powder
- ½ tsp baking soda
- tsp ground cinnamon
- tsp ground nutmeg
- ⅛ tsp ground ginger
- ⅓ cup buttermilk

Method

Drain pineapple, reserving cup juice. Mix pineapple, pecans, 1 tbsp lemon juice, 1 tsp Equal for recipes or 6 packets Equal sweetener and cornstarch in bottom of

8-inch square or 9-inch round cake pan; spread mixture evenly in pan.

Beat margarine and 12 packets Equal sweetener in medium bowl until fluffy; beat in egg. Combine flour, baking powder, baking soda and spices in small bowl. Add to margarine mixture alternately with buttermilk, cup reserved pineapple juice and remaining 1 tbsp lemon juice, beginning and ending with dry ingredients. Spread batter over pineapple mixture in cake pan.

Bake in preheated 350 F oven until browned and toothpick inserted in centre comes out clean after about 25 minutes. Invert cake immediately onto serving plate. Serve warm or at room temperature.

156 calories

www.ingramcontent.com/pod-product-compliance
Lightning Source LLC
Chambersburg PA
CBHW070336230426
43663CB00011B/2347